YOUR KNOWLEDGE HAS VALUE

- We will publish your bachelor's and master's thesis, essays and papers

- Your own eBook and book - sold worldwide in all relevant shops

- Earn money with each sale

Upload your text at www.GRIN.com and publish for free

Isabel Mund

The Advantages and Disadvantages of the British Monarchy in 21st Century Great Britain

GRIN Verlag

Bibliografische Information der Deutschen Nationalbibliothek:

Die Deutsche Bibliothek verzeichnet diese Publikation in der Deutschen Nationalbibliografie; detaillierte bibliografische Daten sind im Internet über http://dnb.d-nb.de/ abrufbar.

Dieses Werk sowie alle darin enthaltenen einzelnen Beiträge und Abbildungen sind urheberrechtlich geschützt. Jede Verwertung, die nicht ausdrücklich vom Urheberrechtsschutz zugelassen ist, bedarf der vorherigen Zustimmung des Verlages. Das gilt insbesondere für Vervielfältigungen, Bearbeitungen, Übersetzungen, Mikroverfilmungen, Auswertungen durch Datenbanken und für die Einspeicherung und Verarbeitung in elektronische Systeme. Alle Rechte, auch die des auszugsweisen Nachdrucks, der fotomechanischen Wiedergabe (einschließlich Mikrokopie) sowie der Auswertung durch Datenbanken oder ähnliche Einrichtungen, vorbehalten.

Imprint:

Copyright © 2013 GRIN Verlag GmbH
Druck und Bindung: Books on Demand GmbH, Norderstedt Germany
ISBN: 978-3-656-57568-9

This book at GRIN:

http://www.grin.com/en/e-book/232705/the-advantages-and-disadvantages-of-the-british-monarchy-in-21st-century

GRIN - Your knowledge has value

Der GRIN Verlag publiziert seit 1998 wissenschaftliche Arbeiten von Studenten, Hochschullehrern und anderen Akademikern als eBook und gedrucktes Buch. Die Verlagswebsite www.grin.com ist die ideale Plattform zur Veröffentlichung von Hausarbeiten, Abschlussarbeiten, wissenschaftlichen Aufsätzen, Dissertationen und Fachbüchern.

Visit us on the internet:

http://www.grin.com/

http://www.facebook.com/grincom

http://www.twitter.com/grin_com

University of Malta
Faculty of Arts
Department of English
Study-Unit: ENG3090 Englishness

The Advantages and Disadvantages of the British Monarchy in 21st Century Great Britain

Handed in by:

Name: Isabel Mund

Total number of words: 1558

Date of submission: 10th June 2013

Introduction

While she was working on the switchboard at the King Edward VII Hospital in London, where the nurses were taking care of Kate Middleton – the Wife of Prince William and Duchess of Cambridge – Jacintha Saldanha, a 46-year-old nurse, became the victim of a hoax call done by two Australian radio DJs in the early days of December 2012. The radio DJs were passing themselves off as the Queen and Prince Charles being worried about the condition of the future King of England's wife. Saldanha put their call through to the duty nurse who therefore provided information about Kate Middleton's condition live on air. Probably as a dramatic result of that call Jacintha Saldanha was found dead two days later[1]. Particularly in such negative situations involving at least one member of the royal family, as happened to Prince Harry very often during the last years[2], one can question the purpose of having a monarchy even if this form of government has become rare in a world which is dominated by the existence of democratic political systems. On the other hand, is not the British monarchy one of the most important and most characteristic features of Great Britain and especially England until today? This essay is not going to discuss the possibilities of abolishing the monarchy as a political institution but it is rather going to list the advantages and disadvantages one can examine – or which are already being examined respectively – when analysing the British monarchy in terms of its influence(s) and importance for the British society.

Advantages: Traditional, Participating, Unifying

The English monarchy is a political institution having a long history and therefore a long tradition as well. In 495[3] this long lasting tradition has already begun. The first king who called himself the "King of the English" was Aethelstan who was crowned in 925[4]. Although the monarchy had to get through partly very difficult centuries – including the rise of the Republicans and therefore critical movements especially from the 19th century onwards[5] – there was not a single point in time at which the monarch was not in charge anymore.

---

[1] http://www.thetimes.co.uk/tto/news/uk/article3624316.ece (accessed 08.06.2013).
[2] See for example http://www.tmz.com/2012/08/21/prince-harry-naked-photos-nude-vegas-hotel-party/ and http://www.guardian.co.uk/media/2005/jan/13/royalsandthemedia.pressandpublishing (both accessed 09.06.2013).
[3] Kenneth J. Panton, *Historical Dictionary of the British Monarchy* (Plymouth: Scarecrow Press, 2011), p. xiii.
[4] Panton, p. xiv.
[5] H. C. G. Matthew, 'The Liberal Age (1851-1914)', in *The Oxford History of Britain*, ed. by Kenneth O. Morgan (Oxford: Oxford University Press, 2001), pp. 518-581 (page 552).

Of course, some laws like for example the Reform Act of 1832[6] have curtailed the political power of the monarchy but never aimed at its complete abolition[7]. Hence, there was always a monarch as the head of government and therefore the English society has somehow got used to this form of government. It has become popular to watch the crowning of a new king, to join his or her funeral and to celebrate a royal wedding like that of Charles and Diana in 1981[8] or that of William and Kate in 2011[9]. Because of the permanent existence of a monarch combined with a non-existence of fundamental critique against the monarchy, this kind of political institution has become a fixed part not only in the political system but also in English society. As has been mentioned above, the political power of nowadays English monarchs is very limited. They can be summarised in the following way:

> [The] king or queen is Head of State. The British monarchy is known as a constitutional monarchy. This means that, while The Sovereign is Head of State, the ability to make and pass legislation resides with an elected Parliament. Although the British Sovereign no longer has a political or executive role, he or she continues to play an important part in the life of the nation. As Head of State, The Monarch undertakes constitutional and representational duties [and] has a less formal role as 'Head of Nation'.[10]

Although the monarch does not have a lot of political power, the opposite is presented in public particularly by the media. An example of this is that the monarch opens the Parliament in a very colourful ceremony that is even broadcasted on television every year[11]. This so-called State Opening is a 'symbolic reminder of the unity of Parliament's three parts: the Sovereign; the House of Lords; and the House of Commons'[12]. When the monarch visits another state[13] or welcomes a foreign minister or ambassador, the English society can participate via internet or television or gets at least informed about it by newspapers. Thus, the English monarch is presented while performing official political acts from time to time and therefore the English society's belief in the political importance of the king or queen gets supported.

As shown above, the English monarchy has a traditional significance in English society. Furthermore, in my opinion the fact of having a common queen or king stabilises the society

---

[6] Matthew, pp. 518-581 (p. 552).
[7] http://www.royal.gov.uk/HistoryoftheMonarchy/KingsandQueensoftheUnitedKingdom/TheHanoverians/WilliamIV.aspx (accessed 09.06.2013).
[8] See for example http://news.bbc.co.uk/onthisday/hi/dates/stories/july/29/newsid_2494000/2494949.stm (accessed 09.06.2013).
[9] See for example http://www.guardian.co.uk/uk/royal-wedding (accessed 09.06.2013).
[10] http://www.royal.gov.uk/MonarchUK/HowtheMonarchyworks/HowtheMonarchyworks.aspx (accessed 06.06.2013).
[11] See an official video of the opening of Parliament in 2009: http://www.royal.gov.uk/ImagesandBroadcasts/ViewFilms/VideoGalleries/Eventsandceremoniesvideogallery.aspx (accessed 09.06.2013).
[12] http://www.parliament.uk/about/faqs/house-of-lords-faqs/lords-stateopening/ (accessed 09.06.2013).
[13] He or she is allowed to do that because of the monarch's role as a Head o State. See http://www.royal.gov.uk/MonarchUK/HowtheMonarchyworks/HowtheMonarchyworks.aspx (accessed 09.06.2013).

as a whole. Because the English monarch is not elected and therefore his or her being the Head of State cannot be supported or prevented by the English people, they are more likely to identify with their queen or king. To put it differently, the monarchy can function as a common ground for the English people because the English monarch does neither represent a specific – or better radical – political aim nor a specific part of society but rather the English – even immigrants – as a whole. This potential stability for the society cannot be reached by another official person be it a political, economical or famous one.

Disadvantages: Expensive, Restricting, Unpopular

When studying the *Forbes List of the Richest Nobles* one can find the current Queen Elizabeth II. at rank 12 owning a capital of approximately 650 million £[14]. Although the royal family can fall back upon such an amount of money, one of the biggest public critiques refers to the enormous expenses caused by the monarchs. The reason is very simple. The monarchs do not use the money they have for paying the costs for example for traveling or for maintaining palaces or other royal buildings. All these things are paid by the state according to a law of 1760[15]. Since these days the British tax payers have to finance the life of their monarchs. In 2012 the amount of money spend every year in the so-called civil list was approximately 32 million £[16]. Other sources even claim that the monarchy produced expenses of 75 million £ a year[17]. The same author also pointed out what this huge amount of money could have been used for as well: 'That [the money spent to finance the lifestyle of the royal family *IM*] would pay the University tuition fees of 75,000 of the poorest students, fund 25 new secondary schools, or pay for the running of an entire hospital'[18]. Although the royal expenses paid by the state did not reach that level last year, 32 million £ are still a big amount of money which could – in fact – be spent for other purposes. While these expenses are a visible and sometimes even noticeable disadvantage of the English monarchy there are some other negative aspects of having an – like in this case – old and traditional monarchial system. Polly Toynbee, an English journalist, explained this specific negative aspect in an interview published in a German newspaper two years ago. She wrote:

---

[14] http://www.forbes.com/2010/07/07/richest-royals-wealth-monarch-wedding-divorce-billionaire.html (accessed 09.06.2013).
[15] http://www.bbc.co.uk/history/british/empire_seapower/acts_of_union_01.shtml (accessed 09.06.2013).
[16] Sir Alan Reid, *Royal Public Finances: Annual Report 2011*-2012. See: http://www.royal.gov.uk/pdf/Financial%20reports%202011-12/75021_Finances%20Section1.pdf (accessed 09.06.2013), p. 1.
[17] http://members.shaw.ca/len92/abolish_monarchy.htm (accessed 09.06.2013).
[18] http://members.shaw.ca/len92/abolish_monarchy.htm (accessed 09.06.2013).

> 'The cultural impact of the monarchy is still immense. Deeply rooted in the British soul are these thoughts and images which are based on the old feudal system and saying that everybody is just a servant and not an equal citizen of a republic. […] Watching the Queen [...] pushes the people back into the era of Empires and into a world which is particularly based on fictitious national myths. […] Other European states, which suffered from invasion, occupation, conquest and defeat during the last century, have managed to start something new, to find new democratic identities and to break with their past. Great Britain has not done this. The monarchy is not a symbol of change'[19].

What Toynbee describes is a psychological restriction resulting from the existence of this social elite which can only be entered by marriage or birth. Hence, the British monarchical system is criticised to be the counterpart of an open and therefore modern society.

These two opinions presented are accumulating in a statistical phenomenon. It seems that the popularity of the English monarchy is decreasing – at least in English society. Although royal sites like the Buckingham Palace still are very popular for tourists from all over the world the British start to dislike their monarchs. This becomes evident in two points. On the one hand, some surveys show that the royals' popularity is shrinking. While in 2007 nearly 19% of the British said that Great Britain would be better off without the monarchs this number increased up to 23% in 2011[20]. On the other hand one can observe a rising republican movement in Great Britain proclaiming the country's turnover to a republic – including the end of the British monarchy[21].

Conclusion

In sum, as shown, the British monarchy is a very traditional institution which fulfils its limited political competencies. Moreover, the British monarchy stabilises the whole society by being a common identification for every Britain. On the other hand, one can argue that the royal system causes a lot of expenses which are financed by public resources. Furthermore, the monarchy is a symbol for an old and restricting social system not representing an ideal open society. All these observations are also recognized by the British society itself. Hence, the popularity of the British monarchy has already started to decrease.

---

[19] http://www.zeit.de/gesellschaft/zeitgeschehen/2011-04/britische-monarchie-kritik/seite-2 (accessed 08.06. 2013 and translated by Isabel Mund).
[20] Compare the figures given in http://news.bbc.co.uk/2/hi/uk_news/7162649.stm and in http://www.guardian.co.uk/uk/2012/may/24/queen-diamond-jubilee-record-support (both accessed 09.06.2013).
[21] http://www.zeit.de/gesellschaft/zeitgeschehen/2011-04/britische-monarchie-kritik/seite-2 (accessed 08.06. 2013).

List of Works Cited

Matthew, H. C. G., 'The Liberal Age (1851-1914)', in *The Oxford History of Britain*, ed. by Kenneth O. Morgan (Oxford: Oxford University Press, 2001), pp. 518-581

Panton, Kenneth J., *Historical Dictionary of the British Monarchy* (Plymouth: Scarecrow Press, 2011)

Reid, Sir Alan, *Royal Public Finances: Annual Report 2011*-2012. See: http://www.royal.gov.uk/pdf/Financial %20reports%202011-12/75021_Finances%20Section1.pdf (accessed 09.06.2013)

http://members.shaw.ca/len92/abolish_monarchy.htm (accessed 09.06.2013)

http://news.bbc.co.uk/2/hi/uk_news/7162649.stm (accessed 09.06.2013)

http://news.bbc.co.uk/onthisday/hi/dates/stories/july/29/newsid_2494000/2494949.stm (accessed 09.06.2013)

http://www.bbc.co.uk/history/british/empire_seapower/acts_of_union_01.shtml (accessed 09.06.2013)

http://www.forbes.com/2010/07/07/richest-royals-wealth-monarch-wedding-divorce-billionaire.html (accessed 09.06.2013)

http://www.guardian.co.uk/media/2005/jan/13/royalsandthemedia.pressandpublishing (accessed 09.06.2013)

http://www.guardian.co.uk/uk/2012/may/24/queen-diamond-jubilee-record-support (accessed 09.06.2013)

http://www.guardian.co.uk/uk/royal-wedding (accessed 09.06.2013)

http://www.parliament.uk/about/faqs/house-of-lords-faqs/lords-stateopening/ (accessed 09.06.2013)
http://www.royal.gov.uk/HistoryoftheMonarchy/KingsandQueensoftheUnitedKingdom/TheHanoverians/ WilliamIV.aspx (accessed 09.06.2013)

http://www.royal.gov.uk/ImagesandBroad-casts/ViewFilms/VideoGalleries/Eventsandceremoniesvideogallery.aspx (accessed 09.06.2013)

http://www.royal.gov.uk/MonarchUK/HowtheMonarchyworks/HowtheMonarchyworks.aspx (accessed 06.06.2013)

http://www.thetimes.co.uk/tto/news/uk/article3624316.ece (accessed 08.06.2013).

http://www.tmz.com/2012/08/21/prince-harry-naked-photos-nude-vegas-hotel-party/ (accessed 09.06.2013)

http://www.zeit.de/gesellschaft/zeitgeschehen/2011-04/britische-monarchie-kritik/seite-2 (accessed 08.06.2013 and translated by Isabel Mund)

CPSIA information can be obtained
at www.ICGtesting.com
Printed in the USA
LVIC06l943070720
659993LV00005B/28